EYE SPY!

I SPY

LETTERS

BY MARIE ROESSER

Gareth Stevens
PUBLISHING

first concepts

I spy letters!

I spy A.

I spy B.

I spy C.
I spy D.
I spy E.

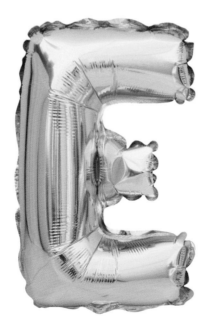

I spy F.
I spy G.

I spy H.

I spy I.

I spy J.
I spy K.

11

I spy L.
I spy M.
I spy N.

I spy O.
I spy P.

15

I spy Q.
I spy R.
I spy S.

I spy T.
I spy U.
I spy V.

I spy W.

I spy X.

21

I spy Y
I spy Z.

When Mayfield joined Cleveland in 2018, he became a source of hope for the team and its fans. As a two-time college walk-on who became the NFL's top draft pick, he had proved he was a special player. Maybe he was special enough to lead the Browns to the playoffs.

Cleveland's 2018 season began like many recent seasons. After nine games, the Browns had an ugly 2–6–1 record. But as Mayfield became more comfortable in the NFL, the team played better. In game 10

Mayfield threw 22 touchdowns in 2019.

Mayfield (*left*) and teammates celebrate after a touchdown in 2018.

against the Atlanta Falcons, he threw three touchdown passes to win. He threw four scoring passes the next week to help the Browns beat the Cincinnati Bengals. The team's defense played better too, holding most opponents to 20 points or fewer. The Browns finished the year 7–8–1.

In 2019, hopes were high in Cleveland. But once again, the Browns fell out of the playoff chase early in the season and couldn't recover. Mayfield knows he will be judged by his team's success in the NFL, not by what he did in college. "You have to hit the reset button," he said. "What I've done in the past doesn't matter." For Mayfield and the Browns, the future is looking much brighter than the past.

Mayfield looks forward to more success on the field.

All-Star Stats

New York Giants running back Saquon Barkley won the 2018 NFL Offensive Rookie of the Year award. But many people thought the prize should have gone to Mayfield. He had one of the best seasons for a rookie quarterback in league history.

Most Touchdown Passes by a Rookie in NFL History

Player	Touchdown Passes	Year
Baker Mayfield	27	2018
Peyton Manning	26	1998
Russell Wilson	26	2012
Andrew Luck	23	2012
Dak Prescott	23	2016
Jim Kelly	22	1986
Butch Songin	22	1960
Jameis Winston	22	2015
Derek Carr	21	2014
Cam Newton	21	2011

Glossary

auction: a sale of something to the highest bidder

conference: a group of teams that play against one another

drill: an exercise designed to improve a skill

endorse: to recommend a product or service, usually in exchange for money

Heisman Trophy: an annual award given to college football's most outstanding player

interceptions: passes caught by the opposing team that result in a change of possession

off-season: the part of a year when a sports league is inactive

scholarships: money to help students pay for school

varsity: the top team at a school

walk-on: a college athlete who tries out for an athletic team without having been recruited or offered a scholarship

10 Tim Keown, "All He Needs Is Hate," ESPN, August 15, 2016, http://www.espn.com/espn/feature/story/_/id/17284078 /oklahoma-sooners-qb-baker-mayfield-used-defying-critics.

15 Mary Kay Cabot, "Browns Draft Baker Mayfield No. 1 Overall in 2018 NFL Draft," Cleveland.com, last modified April 27, 2018, https://www.cleveland.com/browns/2018/04 /browns_draft_baker_mayfield_no.html.

22 Courtney Shaw, "Baker Mayfield, Cleveland Quarterback, Helps Charity Raise $110k in 10 Minutes," NBC26, December 12, 2018, https://www.nbc26.com/sports/baker -mayfield-cleveland-quarterback-helps-charity-raise-110k -in-10-minutes.

27 Bill Bender, "Baker Mayfield's Connection to Cleveland Grows Heading into Exciting Offseason," Sporting News Australia, February 2, 2019, https://www.sportingnews .com/au/nfl/news/baker-mayfield-cleveland-browns-2019 -offseason-afc-playoff-contenders/17o144s0hcftp1v9yn gkwvq9a2.

Further Information

Baker Mayfield
https://bakermayfield.com

Cleveland Browns
https://www.clevelandbrowns.com/

Coleman, Ted. *Baker Mayfield: Football Superstar*. Mendota Heights, MN: Press Room Editions, 2019.

Fishman, Jon M. *Christian Yelich*. Minneapolis: Lerner Publications, 2020.

Pro Football: Baker Mayfield
https://www.pro-football-reference.com/players/M/MayfBa00.htm

Whiting, Jim. *Cleveland Browns*. Mankato, MN: Creative Education, 2019.

Index

Photo Acknowledgments

Image credits: Jason Miller/Getty Images, p. 4; Kirk Irwin/Getty Images, pp. 6, 17, 27; Nick Cammett/Diamond Images/Getty Images, pp. 7, 15, 24, 25, 26; Jamie Sabau/Getty Images, p. 8; mark reinstein/Shutterstock.com, p. 9; JoeSAPhotos/Shutterstock.com, p. 10; wavebreakmedia/Shutterstock.com, p. 11; John E. Moore III/Getty Images, p. 12; Ronald Martinez/Getty Images, p. 13; Jeff Zelevansky/Getty Images, p. 14; Frank Jansky/Icon Sportswire/Getty Images, p. 16; Joe Robbins/Getty Images, p. 18; Matt Winkelmeyer/Getty Images, p. 19; Jerritt Clark/Getty Images, p. 20; Will Powers/Icon Sportswire/Getty Images, p. 21; Rich Polk/Getty Images, p. 22; Justin Edmonds/Getty Images, p. 23.

Cover: Ric Tapia/Icon Sportswire/Getty Images.

Please visit our website, www.garethstevens.com. For a free color catalog of all our high-quality books, call toll free 1-800-542-2595 or fax 1-877-542-2596.

Library of Congress Cataloging-in-Publication Data
Names: Roesser, Marie, author.
Title: I spy letters / Marie Roesser.
Description: New York : Gareth Stevens Publishing, 2022. | Series: Eye spy!
Identifiers: LCCN 2020013441 | ISBN 9781538262511 (library binding) | ISBN 9781538262498 (paperback) | ISBN 9781538262504 (6 Pack) | ISBN 9781538262528 (ebook)
Subjects: LCSH: English language–Alphabet–Juvenile literature. | Alphabet books–Juvenile literature. | Picture puzzles–Juvenile literature.
Classification: LCC PE1155 .R625 2022 | DDC 421/.1–dc23
LC record available at https://lccn.loc.gov/2020013441

First Edition

Published in 2022 by
Gareth Stevens Publishing
111 East 14th Street, Suite 349
New York, NY 10003

Designer: Katelyn E. Reynolds
Editor: Therese Shea

Photo credits: Cover, p. 1 Studio.G photography/Shutterstock.com; cover, back cover, p. 1 (blue background) Irina Adamovich/Shutterstock.com; p. 3 (A) ideabug/E+/Getty Images; p. 3 (B) AlexLMX/ iStock / Getty Images Plus; p. 5 (C) leonard_c/E+/Getty Images; p. 5 (D) Nattawut Lakjit / EyeEm/Getty Images; p. 5 (E) Khuruchon Chanthanyakorn / EyeEm/ Getty Images; p. 7 (F) polesnoy/ iStock / Getty Images Plus; p. 7 (G) Vladimir Nenov / EyeEm/Getty Images; p. 9 (H) imagestock/ iStock / Getty Images Plus; p. 9 (I) koya79/ iStock / Getty Images Plus; p. 11 (J) xxmmxx/ iStock / Getty Images Plus; p. 11 (K) yuriz/ iStock / Getty Images Plus; p. 13 (L) Jamroen Jaiman / EyeEm/Getty Images; p. 13 (M) Samohin/ iStock Editorial / Getty Images Plus; p. 13 (N) KathyDewar/E+/Getty Images; p. 15 (O) Géza Bálint Ujvárosi / EyeEm/Getty Images; p. 15 (P) nantonov/ iStock / Getty Images Plus; p. 17 (Q) gorica/ iStock / Getty Images Plus; p. 17 (R) Queensbury/ iStock / Getty Images Plus; p. 17 (S) Ni Chnan Thn Wngkh Tha Pa / EyeEm/Getty Images; p. 19 (T) pjohnson1/E+/Getty Images; p. 19 (U) mattjeacock/ iStock / Getty Images Plus; p. 19 (V) GEMINI PRO STUDIO/ iStock / Getty Images Plus; p. 21 (W) poplasen/ iStock / Getty Images Plus; p. 21 (X) pagadesign/E+/Getty Images; p. 23 (Y) bzanchi/ iStock / Getty Images Plus; p. 23 (Z) Дмитрий Ларичев / iStock / Getty Images Plus.

Printed in the United States of America

Some of the images in this book illustrate individuals who are models. The depictions do not imply actual situations or events.

CPSIA compliance information: Batch #CWGS22: For further information contact Gareth Stevens, New York, New York at 1-800-542-2595.

Find us on